ONE STILL THING

Nell Regan

ONE STILL THING

ENITHARMON PRESS

First published in 2014
by Enitharmon Press
10 Bury Place
London WC1A 2JL

www.enitharmon.co.uk

Distributed in the UK by
Central Books
99 Wallis Road
London E9 5LN

ISBN: 978-1-910392-04-1

Enitharmon Press gratefully acknowledges the financial support of
Arts Council England, through Grants for the Arts.

British Library Cataloguing-in-Publication Data.
A catalogue record for this book is available
from the British Library.

Designed in Albertina by Libanus Press
and printed in England by
SRP

ACKNOWLEDGEMENTS

Acknowledgements are due to the editors of the following journals where poems or versions of them appeared: *The Irish Times, Southword, Cyphers, Iowa Review, Florida Review, Burning Bush 2, Philippines Free Press, Fleurs de Lettres.*

The author is very grateful to the The Arts Council/An Chomhairle Ealaíon for a Literature Bursary in 2010; Dún Laoghaire-Rathdown County Council for Arts Awards in 2010 and 2011; the Fulbright Commission for a Scholar Award in 2011 to attend the International Writing Programme, University of Iowa & UC Berkeley and the Centre Cultural Irlandais, Paris for a residency in 2013.

Very special thanks are due to Cathy Henderson for friendship and collaboration on the *Thirty-Six Views of the Sugarloaf*; to Mary Swander for hospitality, help and stories in Iowa and more; Iggy McGovern, Siobhan Campbell, Paula Shields and Joseph Lennon for reading & commenting on early drafts; Marion Casey and Fr. John Riordan for research advice; Anne and Philly Dolan; Peter Target for his insightful editing; Mandy Carroll and Mary Coit for putting me up in New York – Jeremy Tiang, Joel Toledo, Josephine Rowe, Chris Merrill, Zoe Strachen and other IWP colleagues and staff; Daniel, Fán, Maggie and Caro at home and away. And R.

For Ronan

CONTENTS

I

II

III

I

LIFFEY SWIM

The light on my forehead winks mud
as I move along the riverbed
in the 3am settling of the city.

The arc of a bike wheel
reveals itself in a shroud
of fronds and slime.

A lugworm inhales
to the bounce of a lone shout
off the granite of quay walls

where I lay my palm
as a far star exhales
in a speck of mica

which I pick and place
on the outstretched
fingertip of the city.

SANTA FE

For Chris Merrill

The walking rain refuses earth
just stains the air
over rucked and puckered hills.

Puckered as though a thread
had snagged in the mantle,
was yanked horizon-taut.

Horizon tricks the eye, a sea –
long gone – is sighted. A fossil
lightly shifts, remembers tide.

The dead are light – cloud light,
the odour of food will suffice
till they bless us with their rain.

The walking rain refuses earth.

ON FINDING OUT THAT GLASS IS NOT A SOLID
AFTER ALL

That this may be a liquid –
the viscosity of which
bears no relationship

to water or even olive oil –
comes as sting or foil
for the mind which still spills

its overflow on the page
trying to gauge
how this tumbler contains

and *is* fluid. But
what of skylight and splinter?
Windscreen and shatter?

Reason becomes molten,
gathers and folds
like honey spun

at medieval evidence
of leaded glass. A once
clear world drops

then slaps as
dousing in bitter sea might –
is this then what it felt

to learn it was not flat
or worse still,
that it turned around the sun?

'A COMPOSER WALKS THE CATACOMBS . . . '

A composer walks the catacombs
hums each resonance as it travels
through stone, through the stacked
dead in their layers of bone. Every

note, whoop and noise rattles
where marrow no longer resides,
the edge-on thighs of nine
million citizens sucked dry by time.

The hum runs up and down
the scales of vertebrae, moves on
to living quarters above. Each
fleshed-out space a receptacle for sound,

which settles as a composition of bells,
running its roughened tongue along the skyline.

PRINTERS' TYPE

Somewhere still a machine
draws red margins

on a page like this one.
Strung up and dipped

in ink, it is a loom for lines.
A young apprentice scrubs

its colour from his hands,
slicks hair back with pomade

and is ready for the dance.
Hours later his girl exits – sweat

drew out the ink – his palm imprints
her rear. The oncologist too

will guess his job by what
the x-ray will reveal. But that

is years away. For now, head
full of the girl, he returns to a trade

busy marking up his future.

FEEDING THE BIRDS

It'd take the patience
of a sniper or a saint
to gain a bird's trust –

outstretched arms, five months,
and so the perch is complete,
a cupped palm full of crumbs

the shake, the tremor,
of muscle holding its own
hour on hour, each hair alert

then, before a crack
a stilled breathing
steady and steadier

(months in a ditch
the quiver of a leaf, scratch
of whin'd give you away

to patrol stillness)
The pick
of a bird's beak, needle sharp,

on an open palm
retorts
out through

nervous system
through hedgerow
and heart.

I teach mindfulness
these times. How to focus, solely,
on the task to hand.

from THIRTY-SIX VIEWS OF THE SUGARLOAF
for Cathy Henderson

Think waves that peel back the skin
of the sea by Shankill; a re-assemblage
of its aspect from IKEA; the sipping
of Earl Grey at Avoca; or how it sets

off the first fag of the day, in a balcony
scene, hunched against the sky
while a mobile mast scores its every
angled line deep into the print.

Or something seen, in the foreground,
a gesture and the eye is lead beyond
the camber of the sparrow hawk,
that lends its name to the meadow slope

because *His Fuji wasn't the focal*
point, you call, in delight,
and when we look at the (admittedly
poor) repro's of 36 *Views,* it's true;

rather, it's the cresting of that wave
pitching fishermen through spume;
bowed backs on the highway; blossom
sifting time (think May and snowy

falls of hawthorn here); figures
on the teahouse terrace as steam
rises from miso soup; all those
lives lived on and about the peak

that take centre stage. Now I know
its also the workhouse, set in off
the roundabout of the day to day,
reborn as hospital. The mountain

is dumb as x-rays are pulled. There
where light should be (picture
cherry wood carved) through each
bronchial branch, shadow scatters.

Nearby, the M50 bridges Brides Glen,
in a rapid slipstream of metal, a truck
whips up a backwash, a rising falling
screen or caul and above it, one still thing.

LITTORAL

Rain has bitten away much of this month
but left us this foot-lifting morning,
glistening, its evening ahead like an open
palm or attenuated mind. Above us, ridges
where each next-sighted peak promises
renewal, the city a coastling in its bays

and a sight of the sea reveals a father
on the sand, his last child in his arms.
Look. Waves. Waves. Like this, steps

forward and extends his hand so their
wrists flex over thresholds of meaning
and they stand as land and water seam.

SOWN

The hills are buttered with gorse wrote
Eileen's Uncle Johnny, before a freak wind
took, tossed to the sky the whole body

of his shed. *Lucky for me,* he thought,
it wasn't nailed to the floor, or that
would have been that. He sat as overhead

a flock of pages, caught in an updraft
of dispersal, rose over Djouce, Kippure,
Three Rock, then dropped – a lifetime's work

mulched under. The year sped read
its seasons, till gorse was at it again
and from each hill a crop of words had spread.

RENDER

Through the teeth of its limbs
the tree is combing the wind
soothing and smoothing
the salted notes and stringing
them to its own taut form.

Repetition. The sleek air learns
to lie itself on the lean of the reach
of the tree and soon each
branch has stretched out an over arm

and wind become incarnate
as tree, combed through
to a stooped inclination of its own.

ARCHAEOLOGY CLASS

Air is porous in this midge-hungry field,
bog bounded by drystone within
which squats a bath. Great wheels of silage
yearn to turn on invisible axes. A riverbed
rock, scoured, scooped and smooth,
propped in the toppled portal tomb
with its capstone; behemoth, erratic.

It's all words, says one, as we reassemble
with language of cist and corbel, each part
of the dry wall back unto the cairn. Now,
just as they abut each other, that older,
metamorphic tongue seeps through.

WOODCUT

The flat scorper glides
along the lip of branch,
scooping out sky –
an astringency of lime
released and the thrush
sings out, in relief.

Such sure-footed moves
in wood – you a seven-year
apprentice to crutch, to grip
so ligament and intent are one –

the key turns smooth in the lock,
the forest door swings open, wide.

MIST AT DUSK
Pigs' Hollow

Maybe it's the breath
of the giant pig that lay
then rose and moved off
the lea of the hill,
rump swaying, steam
rising, for Snuggery Lane

or maybe it's the breath
light leaves; having pitched up,
settled on the slope, it shrugs
and moves off down
the mountain side as
nights' grasses spring back again.

II

PASSAGE

PROLOGUE

taut

beyond the thought

or horizon of this line

a story unwinds

SECTION 1   HORIZON

DAWN * 1 FEBRUARY * COBH TO NEW YORK

adrift
in
idleness

my hands
in an attitude of confusion
pluck

at my hem
seek fabric
for finger and thumb

to pinch to needle
lick squint
thread

see glint of silver
as now dolphins
loop through wave

seaming
and stitching
the sea

DAY TWO

I am here
nothing to do
nothing to be done

the sun rises
and sets
whatever I do

my head rings
with goodbyes

the crowded cabin

sea ahead
sea behind

horizon

the day is nothing
but horizon
horizon around

abound

even thoughts of him
becalm

DAY THREE

rocking is the motion
I will recall
when I am on soil once more

my fingers curl round
the stone
he gave me

my other hand
grips cold steel
of the railing

anchors me at sea
as far from gone
as near arrival

I am between two lives

DAY FOUR

trousseau

a white edged picture
of the family as I go

and his letter

stitched in the hem of my coat
with notes that crackle as I move

I unpick it once more

Nell a chroí, I'll never get work here with this crowd in
power. The gaffer took one look – signalled your
brother in, me out, knew me for an Irregular. I am
resolved. It is time to head. A cousin in Queens always
said he'd see me right so when we've saved your
passage (if you consent) I'd be made up to have you
here with me. Our own Tír na nÓg across the sea.
I enclose this. Picked on the day trip we took, you
loved the dignity of the grey pebble, nameless amidst
thousands but still vivid as any precious one. For now
keep this as a ring of sorts and I will see you on Ellis.

DAY FIVE

Disembark

the heart's gangplank
descends

SECTION 2 STEEL

Dear Sis,

Two days, two nights
not a sign of him yet.

Where shall I be
when these words reach your eyes?

Under my feet
the ground gives way.

Dear Sis,

You'll ask have I heard? No. Not a word.
Is it one month or two since I left? I forget.
All I know is my eyes were alight for him
but other eyes watched us sign in, file
to climb the stairs. *They watch for shortness*
of breath, a trip, so mind your step, hissed
a woman next to me.

Nothing prepared us
for the scrape of the button hook they took
to inspect our eyes for disease. It scratches
still in my sleep. But I passed the test
so eased past those who were chalked up –
each letter an infirmity, a whole alphabet
stood dumbly by, its head hung for disease.

Four nights I waited by the post, others came
and went. Oh Kitty, he even wrote this out
for me when entreating me to come over
here, where *days pass like a wayward tune.*
Where broken faith has never been known.
Instead I am one of a thousand broken tunes
caught in the throat of this city.

An agent
from the Immigrant Girls brought me off.
He held my elbow as we descended at Battery,
crushed by hawkers, handlers, gawpers
and scrappers, steered me to the Church
of the Holy Rosary, shelter and jobs
for unaccompanied Irish girls provided
you'll do their bidding. I am biding my time.

My old life is smelting down.
The blood in my veins begins
to temper, a steel cage closes
on my core

                      my legs seek bedrock
I sink my footings in the stone
and brace myself.

City of hurried and sparkling waters . . . city nested in bays

WALT WHITMAN

I spend my breaks
on the quays
watch the boats

a cargo of souls
lists in the water

such ballast of
expectation

*

Mad for bridges here
(they are they are)

span for span they span
the bays, the rivers

rivets attaching each
and every one

*

I met a man
turns sky inside out

tell me tell me he says

Dear Sis,

The stories I've heard here you wouldn't
believe, (though, heart ease for me
in some curious way). This – the cook
with her sister, set to collect a third
off Ellis. Found she'd died crossing
over. Imagine that subway ride
back to Brooklyn – silence as deep,

as wide, as any Atlantic tide. Last night
she spat at my longing, *Home? A hard,
a cruel place, if it held 'that' for us,
we wouldn't have left.* So, I work
to count what blessings I have – sick
of the coal-scuttle, sis and my fingers
are wrecked. Its months since I've sewn.

Tell Paddy I come close to forgiveness
for introductions to you-know-who
(any word?) Aside from dreaming a familiar
cap and stride at each corner or fractured
turn, I heard of a young Corkman, works
in the vault of the Federal Reserve,
locked in overnight, emerged raving

about betrayal and failing his girl. They think
Ellis is her name? Who knows . . . or now cares?
I have other news – I've been asked out by
a steel worker, calls himself sky walker,
half-Indian too. I reckon doors will be
shut against us if we do take up. My next
day off, we meet on top of the world.

NOON * 1 MAY * WOOLWORTH TOWER

You are the city's grace
  as you step
the narrow beam of steel.

I want to hear how your soles ache
as you walk out, swinging on a backdrop
of nothing and stinging height – when
we take the sidewalk you track a path
so narrow, I fear we are 500 feet up;
my knees go – a vertigo that turns sky
inside out, opens in the ground a chasm
from which steam issues like flame.

my thoughts
  are a fire escape
zigzagging up

Tell me how you stay immune
to that fusillade of rivet shot
retorting back (or the babble below,
hungry for the place of the fallen)
because, as this city erupts in my ear,
I am but an avenue for klaxon
and horn grating though flesh
and bone, a funnel for its impress.

an elevator breath
  exhales – moves up and down
my diaphragm

Tell me, tell me you say *about the catch*
in your eye . . . Look. Laid out below us,
this thicket of towers that shores onto
the hungry gob of the Hudson, there it is.
Ellis all turreted and Turkish. The island
of gulls you call it, well I tell you,
they were posted atop the pailings
and fixed us with their gimlet eyes.

     imagined
architecture
  has conquered the air

Did he arrive? First, tell me of the tale
your granda dandled you to, of the lost speech
of his tribe, its different words for the self-same
things, if named by a woman or named by a man.
How his father's word for *deer* was not that
which his mother spoke. Tell me again
so I may understand how *See you on Ellis*,
and *He is not here*, became the same.

  red-tailed hawk
    sails past – content on
the canyon's updraft

I am resolved to keep close
to the ground and attend
to small things. A moth
caught in the light
between buildings,
the stain of tea on a coverlet,
the water tower with its spindly legs.
This pearl button I hold in my hand.

  we are in the weather
now – seeking heaven's
floor.

SECTION 3   GOLD

MIDNIGHT * NEW YORK FEDERAL RESERVE VAULT

No dawn down here. No dawn
    in the deep rock of the island.
This rich lode of bricks. All
    handled, hawked from cell
to numbered cell. The vault door
    cumbered like a ship's turn at sea;
its ballast gold. The cylinder
    lifted a quarter inch, sealed me in

eight floors below. Quiet down here.
    Quiet. Who knew bullion could be so still?
Breathless. Resting. Caged. Yet
    the exact calibration of human skin;
its sheen, its lustre, its steady
    lustering. Once to sense a warmth
I took off my glove,
    annealed it as a jeweller would

a lover's palm stroking an arm, a breast,
    my fingertips stirred by what emanates
but the squeal of the trolley's wheel
    takes me back to my day's labour
as according to transactions
    enacted above, we load and unload
gold – we are all brickies down here
    building, unbuilding walls of bullion.

Always use the stone you lift,
    my father said as we stood before
the dry wall, *make it fit.*
    What he would make of this?
A prison for all this wealth. As we trawl
    the trolley underground my companion
told me of gold-beaters skin – gut of ox,
    tenacious, laid out between leaves

of gold as they're hammered to a clarity
    of their own. Night moves on
while I pick at the floor, grasp for air
    though I know we're under water here
fifty feet or more. Boats pass
    overhead, disgorge another cargo
Ellis. Ellis, see you on Ellis, I said
    and throughout the night her eyes

widen. Her mouth's startled hiss.
   This immigrant refers to you ...
And how to explain? That each hour
    was loading itself on the scales?
If you desire to call on her behalf . . .
   That the tip of the clock tower hour hand
quivered as it settled
    on twelve, one, two. . . ? *the ferryboat leaves*

every hour on the hour . . . that it quivered like the needle
  on these scales? That I can live
with myself down here except when it wavers
 as we pile each ingot high, scale
calibrated so fine a feather breath
  might move it, a grain of rice alter it.
Silence as it settles and holds, the inspector nods.
  Can gold breathe? What would a soul's betrayal

weigh in gold? I fancy I hear the molten glister
  or exhale as a finger print gleams on its side.

SECTION 4 SHELL

An agent arrived, seeking Irish girls
for positions Midwest – I
looked at a map, realised
I'd a continent to my back, decided

to face again beyond the island
I was on. Iowa it'd be and well timed
as the man I was doing a line
with unsettled me, wanting to settle down.

*

In my ears, the high-pitched wail,
I am tipped as though the rails
are calling me, my legs go, balance
wavers before I steady, step back
onto the platform bank. I grip my bag
stand straight and let the stream
of strangers open and close around me.

An Angelus resound brings me home.
Dinner steams on the table, mother
checks, *You didn't go near the river*
now? No the dutiful reply, though its lure
increased by the day. The mind's detour
halted by the snort of the train, Chicago-bound.

Dear Paddy, this comes direct from The Pearl
Button Capital of the World (no lie) but a scut
of a place in truth – Muscatine, on the banks
of the wide Mississippi rolling by. Gripped by
a gold rush of its own – mussels they flock here to haul
from the river bed, the mother lode, mother-of pearl.

Imagine Mallow possessed, each alley and street
heaped with middens of discarded cut shell, the rotted
flesh feeds hogs or clogs the drains while day
and night the whine and bite of cutting machines
enters the mind, spitting out button blanks
clouds of dust. Ten thousand tons a year leave here.

The world has become
a button of shell which I stitch to a card.

I work for a family called Barry (Wexford though,
before you get too het up) the Granda apparently
transformed the trade – made a machine that punches
buttons from shells at ferocious speed – big wigs

in this place. At any rate they only like to hire Irish
girls (too many fraulines round here, he says).
I've taken in piece work for my evenings off
though I walk too – this flat place recedes

both ways, not a hill in sight, I love the river,
its wide and muddied water, I see the faded
chart of the classroom wall, know the sharp sting
of the stick, hear *Four i's four s's two p's. Repeat.*

They're down a hand in the factory so I'm to be sent.
Fine pay to be had, if I can handle the stench.

P.S. I'll send on what I can.

STORY

Boepple, bathing in the Mississippi,
cut his foot on a mussel shell. He knew
his buttons this fella, knew fresh water
shells inlaid with mother-of-pearl were ideal

– thus was Muscatine reborn as capital
of the world (at least in pearl button terms).
Fast forward two decades – see Boepple
again. Bathing in the Mississippi. Cutting

his foot on a mussel shell. Infection races
through his blood this time. He dies.
Not often you get to say shell is both
the making and the death of the man.

*

Dear Paddy, I know it's said you can't step
in the same river twice – but you should mind
the clammers here, each man, woman and child
foots it in and out of her shallows and depths

ten hours a day or more. These mussels make
the best buttons or so I'm told; the Pimpleback,
Fat Pocketbook and Three ridged Mucket
(whatever a mucket is). Two things I cannot forget

happened last week. First, I found, hidden fast
in the factory this – 'Being the Story
of the Button Workers' Strike led by one Pearl
McGill'. Thirteen years back but still it seems

taboo. Asked my neighbour, another sorter,
did she know her, this young Pearl?
(and was that really her name?) *Muckracker*
she bit back at me and snapped

shut. Her daughter was shot
in the strike, died at the hands of the National
Guard. Some price to pay for a button. And one
her young man will never get to open.

Then this: the Barrys' aged uncle came
to dine, swinging in his chair, red faced,
all yap of wars past, of buffalo
rotting in the sun. The adults yawn

and make polite, tinkle cut glass. Good folk
round here do not boast, their down cast faces
say. The children sit up though, bright-eyed
Tell us again uncle – how you scalped that squaw.

STORY

A whole townland from Mayo
makes it out on a ship. A new start
as blight lays waste to each narrow
drill. Headed west they start

to find gold, black gold to be tilled
the rich topsoil of Osceola County,
say, Iowa. They may have tipped
the soil on their heads, fallen to

their knees, rubbed their faces
in its sweetness then sowed
and reaped and sowed once more.
Gathering on the horizon like a code

they have no key for or a *sidhe gaoithe*
a swarm of grasshoppers ticks.
That winter famine sweeps them up
in her bony arms. Sniggers.

My dreams are of sorting, sifting seeds
and specks which then begin to mix once
more. I pick as though my thumb and fore-
finger are stuck fast or clasped together.

I think I wake, a heavy sack on my back
a cramp in my big toe, my calf cut in two
locked, bent back as if possessed by one
not I, but then am awakened by a cough

which is my own, from deep in the dust bowl
of my lungs and come to, on another black night
alone, trapped in the shell of my mind
or the mind of my shell. I am the piece of grit

caught, that each day layers and accretes
itself over, until there is nothing of me left.

STORY

Or the woman who journeys
west to the land of the living
and on to the Great Plain
only to find she is dying.
In her hand a mussel shell
opens like a pair of lungs
slices finger, red pumps, she runs
to a nurse, who staunching it tells

her her cough is more the thing
·as it speckles kerchief and coverlet
with blood. Suggests sanatorium:
Your only chance is to stay put and rest.

That day she sets her course for home.
Despite advice, a passage must be earned.

*

As night weans the moon
the river is lit by shell
so I dream in shell
dreaming what mussels
dream — seams of dusky light
pearl the roof of my skull
so the sky is a skull
where dusk dreams
of pearling reflected moons
as they river through shell
and mother-of-dusk becomes daughter-
of-pearl. and I dream a coracle

that would sail me home
down the spine of America.

SECTION 5 NIGHT

1 NOVEMBER * NEW YORK TO COBH

                I look
out to the bridge through which
I will pass. My ticket home
stamped, stitched in the hem
of my coat.

                Barges
boast in the harbour, acrid oil
soaks the air as the engine vibrates
and runs through me. Any receding
place seems sad and what of the self
left there? Bombarded by its sight
and sound.

             Seagulls in the wake
of the boat criss-cross the white foam
and the skyscrapers – those towers
and palaces I first saw – recede.
Our Lady of the Harbour bless me.
The sun glints, gluts on a torch
on any hope of a new reach.

            The gulls keep abreast
of the boat now, each departing
wingbeat as I drop the pebble
into the water. Daredevil it gathers

all the noise back into itself like
a box repacking – or the restitching
of a body after an operation.

The seagulls turn for land.

NIGHT ONE

I drift
in

uneasy sleep

I wake
in

the offing

NIGHT TWO

no one returns
from

Tír na n-Óg

not even with tales
of sky-tipped cities

whose light
consoles the stars

NIGHT THREE

like looking
up

into ocean depths

a tower
sinks

through earth and sky

some inner axis

NIGHT FOUR

the water rises

my dreams
are caulked

NIGHT FIVE

I am returned.

Off the cleated
gang plank

I stumble.

III

PRAIRIE DAYS

The day shakes out the towel
of its morning on the prairie

where the curious insect
and quaking grass

are poised to listen.

*

Come, let us raise dust
on dirt roads and later,

when we whisper, muster
a silence that might yet

make flesh of itself.

*

The tree cups sky
in its palm

as a child suckles
in its shade.

*

The bed of my afternoon
would willingly

unmake
itself for you.

IOWA CITY SESTINA

This town is stitched by river –
that finds and winds its way through trees
whose leaves curl yellow and every poem
is found to contain it, them and cicada
call – perhaps they too stand for longing
forded by an imagined Atlantic bridge.

Outside my window the bridge
of green, wrought iron spans the river
asks *What is there to miss?* It will not be long
love, till you find me under this tree
straining to describe the cicada
song that is shot though this poem.

Each avenue of the city, a walking poem
of considered views that yield to bridges
over which the chatter and clatter of cicada
curls and pulls time forward in a river-
ing flow while leaf considers tree
and the blue reflection of sky is longing

for river just as water is longing
for colour much as word yearns for poem
or its echo in a lover's ear. The tree
stands alone, says *Desire less*, bridge
with what you have here and the river
will carry to you all the cicada

pulse and call of a continent. Wish cicada
tymbal on the banks of all Iowas along
the Mississippi as it rivers
out through prairie, plain and poem.
The pitched sough of the train that bridges
the night, freights stories of cornfield, of oak tree

to the city's gridded morning where trees
anoint the grass with shade, students read, cicada
conversations fade. Later, stepping to the bridge
the Capitol dome will throw its gold reflection, elong-
ating the reach of a September dusk where a poem
or thought might constellate. Deep in the river

open-mouthed carp gape up at trees, long
branches pooling on its ceiling while cicada-poem
clicks, calls forth a silent bridge to span the river.

JET LAG

Through the narrow aisles of my sleep
a trolley rocks as night delays over land,
new found, and the lip of my dream seeks

yours. I stretch and reach for your hand
but altitude drops as my lungs still exhale
the stale breath of one hundred strangers

who are inhaling mine. I see why they say
the psyche or spirit can't travel at this speed
that it lags behind at a walking or sailing

pace. Mine gathers someplace (last week
perhaps) and this morning would
tip the sky to let sunlight flood and reach

your co-ordinates on the globe, as your words
reach my screen, so many spilling stars.

TRIPTYCH

In this venn diagram of a shared life
(two circles that overlap) their inter

section blooms – wild seeding
the eclipsed moon of each self alone.

*

See the moon's ascent
before a monthly wane

when time hinges on its turn
and all is interior again.

*

All blaze and black Madonna
I take my place before her:

Guide my life, I entreat
Live it! she retorts.

GIFTED

It's the movement of rock in the molten core
and the hair's breadth shift of the moon
that has foxed the atomic pulse of *caesium*

(that element, accurate to some number further
than the furthest planet, its root the Latin
for *sky blue*; I can see it in December's clear roof

as we undertake our pilgrimage back to sun)
and so its clock gifts an extra second to our year.
May it drop like a pebble in the lake of itself,

be as subtle an alteration as a beat
before the reptilian brain reacts,
an extra breath that gathers

more seconds or, may it be
that silent moment of conception.

'I PARSE THE SOIL . . . '

I parse the soil
to find the seeds
that did not germinate;

one, its white tail
trails off like
a question mark.

(An *imperfect*
process, the
doctor kindly says.)

I watch the tiny
fists of other
leaves unfurl.

SONG

Our lying still

is the white page
upon which
this poem

settles.

*

In the blue-blush
of a February dusk
light returns –

like absent scent.

*

I am taking my lessons
in passion
from fuschia –

her skirts lift up

each drop of honey
exults.

SILENCE

Seeking purchase on the balcony rail
Finding the solemn note of the steel girder

Damping into wooden boards
As little symphonies splutter on the tin chair,

The rain is falling, picking out
Each surface and calling it back;

If a poem displaces the weight
Of its sound in water

Then let these loosened drops
Brim out over the edge of night

Evaporate and fall again
To call back a sonar image

Of where I lie, without you,
And let a singing line begin.

LIEDER

Here is a little song to comfort you.
Sing it to yourself softly, simply, just as you are.
Robert Schumann to Clara Schumann, July 1840

His scent still rose off my skin.
My pores exuded the impress of his hand
and my throat whimpered want, when
the bouquet of songs arrived, bound
by a single chord which I plucked, spilling
sheaves, all their cadent, radiant content.

I *his rapture*, I *his pain*. He mine.
He said light hit the water like a cadenza
that day, but his soul could not resist
the shadows of the bridge, its counter melody.
Now, as behind me each door slams, bolts,
I only meet what beats in him

in the tremolo of my larynx
or the dark corridor of the keyboard.

TEST

In the tightly plotted garden of our estate,
a crop has ripened overnight;
a ball buds in the apple tree, a doll
blooms in the azalea's arms
while grass is spattered, beds are brilliant
with the fruits of next doors' twins'

abandon. These thin walls often give
on rows, on three-year-old footfall of intent,
and must too on our lovemaking
at certain times of the month –
all nosing toward a future in long,
narrow boats of rooms. But now,

loosening the need for a one result,
is the windfall of our laughter as we look out.

BAY AREA

See! I am dancing!
On the rim of the world I am dancing.
                                        Ohlone

The tiny feet of the rain dance
on the slant roof of my sleep
all night they tap out a beat –
a rhythm that gathers pace

to itself, then fades, builds
up once more in echo
to the waves that fall where
pacific meets shore.

The morning mist clears
and through the open door
of skype, the time lapse
of your lips, I thought

I might slip through to
our bed to inhale your scent,
settle a bit before return.
Instead I am on the edge

of the world looking out –
eight hours from home
in the embrace of the
enormous arm of the bay.

'RAIN HAS LOOSENED ITSELF . . . '

Rain has loosened itself from the sky
and overhead become intimate
with scent, with song, with the sigh

of a branch brushed by the beat
of a wood pigeon's wing. So,
before we set our glasses down

these plump minutes on the sofa,
looking out at lengthening dusk,
demand a grammar of their own,

making as they do a cover of last light
under which we call and respond,
translate the what-has-been into a yet-to-come.